Sight-Word Stories

ALTERNATIVE STRATEGIES FOR EMERGENT READERS

by
Gloria Lapin

FEARON TEACHERS AIDS
A Division of Frank Schaffer Publications, Inc.

EDITOR
Susan Eddy

DESIGNER
Ruth Otey

ILLUSTRATOR
Jody Jobe

COVER PHOTOGRAPH
Michael Gaffney

This Fearon Teacher Aids product was formerly manufactured and distributed by American Teaching Aids, Inc., a subsidiary of Silver Burdett Ginn, and is now manufactured and distributed by Frank Schaffer Publications, Inc. FEARON, FEARON TEACHER AIDS and the FEARON balloon logo are marks used under license from Simon & Schuster, Inc.

© **Fearon Teacher Aids**
A Division of Frank Schaffer Publications, Inc.
23740 Hawthorne Boulevard
Torrance, CA 90505-5927

ISBN 1-56417-670-3

7 8 9 MAL 01 00

Contents

Introduction

ABOUT SIGHT-WORD STORIES

A warm welcome to teachers and parents of young readers! This reproducible collection of controlled-vocabulary books is designed for emergent readers. The focus is on frequent repetition of a small sampling of sight words. Pictures are designed to provide needed clues. These books help young readers whose learning style may be whole word rather than phonetic.

If you are using these books with your own children, be sure to make the experience of reading a pleasant one by picking a time when you can work at a leisurely pace, without interruptions. Think of each book as a journey to be completed in small steps. Avoid the temptation of trying to do too much at once.

ASSEMBLING AND USING THE BOOKS

Sight-Word Stories are designed to be photocopied by adults, and cut apart and collated by children. Of course, if you prefer, you may do the entire assembly yourself.

1. Cut pages apart along the dotted lines.

2. Assemble pages in numerical order.

3. Staple the book in the upper left corner or along the left side of the cover.

Once a book is assembled, point to the words as you read the title. Then invite children to do the same. If they have not yet seen the pictures, ask children to predict what will be inside the book. Open and enjoy the pictures together. Ask lots of questions about the pictures to encourage development of oral language skills. After exploring the pictures together, say the words. Then encourage young readers to point to the words while saying them. The *point and say* process is important. It helps beginning readers follow a story while establishing the connection between sight and sound.

Direct attention to words that appear both with initial capital letters and initial lowercase letters. Explain that the first letter may look different but the word is the same. If a child forgets a previously presented word while working on a new book, speak encouragingly. Pull out the earlier book in which the word was presented. Invite the child to review the familiar book, find and identify the word, and apply it to its new setting.

Reread the book and reward children by inviting them to color the pictures. This reinforces ownership of the text. Encourage children to read a book several times over a three to five day period. Repetition moves the words into long-term memory. You may wish to help young readers make new books similar to the one just read by having them dictate stories to you. Children may then create original drawings to accompany the stories you have printed. You may also wish to do some of the activities that follow.

FOLLOW-UP ACTIVITIES USING WORD CARDS

1. After reading a book at least twice, present the appropriate word cards (see pages 61–63). Cards are marked with corresponding book numbers. Review newly learned words *after* the story so that they are first learned in context. Words used only once in the story are not included in the cards.

2. Present one word at a time. Invite children to find that word in the story and then say the word. Have them identify several places where the word appears. Place all the familiar word cards on the table and play "Find It" by asking children to find a certain word and hold it up. Continue until all the words in a story have been identified.

3. Create new sentences using the word cards.

4. Make two copies of word cards and play "Go Fish" by mixing and dealing out four cards to each player. The rest are stacked in a pile. Player 1 asks for a word card that will match one in his or her hand. If the other players do not have that card, they respond, "Go Fish." Player 1 then picks a card from the top of the pile and Player 2 asks for a matching word. Whenever a player creates a pair of word cards, the set is placed face up on the table. When a player has matched all his or her cards and has none left, that player takes a new card from the pile so that the game may continue until all the words are matched.

FOLLOW-UP ACTIVITIES USING PHONICS

Now that children have learned some sight words, these words can be used to learn other words. For example, ask children to look at the word *run* and say the word. Then ask what would happen if you replaced the *r* with an *s*. Write the word *sun* under the word *run* to help children recognize it. If a child is hesitant, guide him or her by saying, "*Run* turns into *s— —*" (supply the *s* sound). If a child is not developmentally ready for this approach, you may wish to read the appropriate list of four words below and have the child repeat them. After enough repetition, children will be able to read the list. Let each child's developmental level determine how quickly you proceed with this technique.

run	can	hot	sit	ride	sat	like
sun	tan	pot	bit	side	pat	bike
fun	man	not	fit	hide	mat	hike
bun	pan	lot	hit	tide	hat	Mike

OTHER ACTIVITIES

Invite children to dictate stories. These may be written as little books that children illustrate or written on easel paper. Children may use pointers while reading stories aloud. Try covering several words in the story with blank cards and asking children to figure out the missing words through memory or context clues.

The text of any story may be copied onto sentence strips. The strips can be mixed up for children to reorder. Blank cards may be used to cover a word in each sentence or a beginning letter. Children may supply the missing sounds and name the missing letters.

Sentence strips may be cut into words for children to reassemble one sentence at a time. Children may refer back to the original story or try to reconstruct the sentence from memory. Cut-apart words can also be reassembled into new sentences or used to study word families, such as the rhyming words on pages 62–63.

Vocabulary List

The following words appear at least twice in the books in which they are found.

Book 1

A
is
big
little

Book 2

Are
you
my
baby
No
Yes
My

Book 3

You
are
not
mother

Book 6

Run
run
In
Out
out

Book 7

up
down
in
Hot
dog

Book 8

Boys
Girls
ride
Ride
jump
Jump
and

Book 9

girl
sat
on
the
swing
boy
rabbit
mouse
They
fell

Book 10

I
like
dogs
can
Dogs
Big
Little
sit
to

Book 11

The
got
box

Book 12

am
a
read
Can
walk

Book 15

will
house
He
get
bike
go
too
We

Book 16

Father
likes
Mother
Baby
cannot

Book 17

pig
has
of

Book 18

She
books
reads
book

Book 19

There
bear
cat

Book 20

wants
race
line
say
says

Book 1

BIG
AND
LITTLE

A house is big.

2

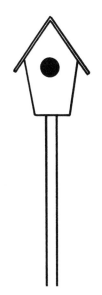

A birdhouse is little.

3

A bear is big.

4

A mouse is little.

5

A jet is big.

6

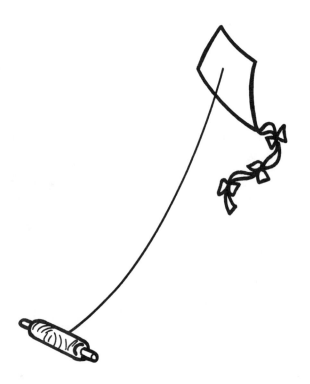

A kite is little.

7

A tree is big.
A flower is little.

8

Book 2

BABY
BABY

Are you my baby?

No.

2

Are you my baby?

No.

3

Are you my baby?

Yes!

4

Are you my baby?

No.

5

Are you my baby?

No.

6

Are you my baby?

Yes!

My baby!

My baby!

12

7

8

Book 3

MOTHER AND BABY

You are not my mother.

2

You are not my mother.

3

You are my mother!
Yes. You are my baby.

4

13

You are not my mother.

5

You are not my mother!

6

You are my mother!
Yes. You are my baby.

7

You are my baby.

8

14

Book 4

ARE YOU BIG?

Are you big? Yes.

2

My mother is big.

3

Are you big? Yes.

4

15

My mother is big.

5

Are you big? Yes.

6

My mother is big.

7

My mother is big.

8

Book 5

ARE YOU LITTLE?

Are you little?

Yes.

2

My baby is little.
3

Are you little?

Yes.

4

17

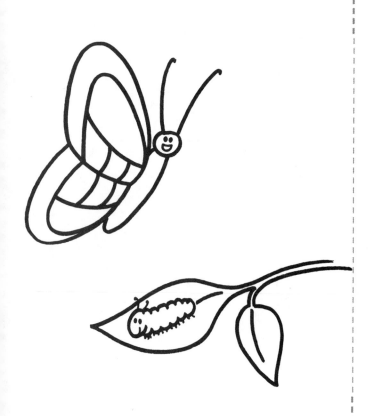

My baby is little.

5

Yes.

6

My baby is little.

7

My baby is little.

8

Book 6

Run, run.

2

Run, run. In.

3

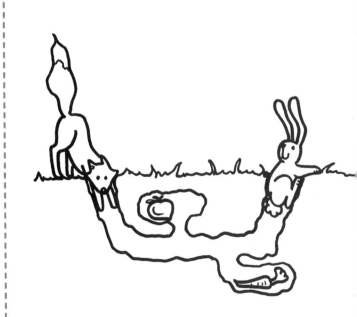

In. Out.

4

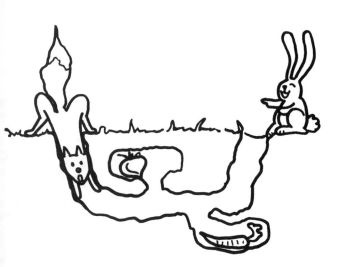

In. Out.

5

Out. In.

6

In. Run out.

7

Out. In.

8

Book 7

UP AND DOWN

Run, run. Run up.

2

Run, run. Run down.

3

Run, run. Run up.
Run, run. Run down.

4

21

Run up.
Run down.
Run in. Run, run.

5

Run out.
Run in.
In, out, up, down.
Run, run.

6

Up, down, in, out.
Run up. Run down.
Run in. Run out.

7

Hot dog!

8

Book 8

BOYS RUN

Girls run.
Run, girls, run.
2

Boys ride.
Ride, boys, ride.
3

Girls ride.
Ride, girls, ride.
4

23

Boys jump.
Jump, boys, jump.

5

Girls jump.
Jump, girls, jump.

6

Boys and girls run.
Run in, boys and girls.

24

7

Girls and boys ride.
Ride out, boys and girls.

8

Book 9

THE SWING

A girl sat on the swing.

2

A boy sat on the swing.

3

A rabbit sat on
the swing.

4

25

A bear sat on
the swing.

5

An eagle sat on
the swing.

6

A mouse sat on
the swing.

7

The swing broke.
They fell down.

8

Book 10

DOGS

I like dogs.
I like big dogs.

2

I like dogs.
I like little dogs.

3

Dogs can run.
Big dogs run.
Little dogs run.

4

Dogs can jump.
Big dogs jump.
Little dogs jump.

5

Dogs run up.
Dogs run down.

6

Dogs jump up.
Dogs jump down.

7

Dogs can sit.
I like dogs to sit.
Big dogs sit.
Little dogs sit.

8

28

Book II

THE BOX

The sheep got on
the box.

2

The pig got on
the sheep.

3

The pig got two balls.

4

29

The cat got on the pig.

5

The bird got on the cat.

6

The spider got on
the bird.

7

The fly got on
the spider.

8

Book 12

I LIKE TO READ

I am a little girl.
I like to run in and out.
I like to jump up and down.
I like to ride and ride.

2

I am a big girl.
I like to sit and read.
I like to read to you.
I like to read to
the baby.

3

I am a little boy.
I like to run to
my mother.

4

31

I like to run to my dog.
I like to jump up
and down.

5

I am a big boy.
I sat down. I got up.
Are you a big boy?

6

I can walk.
I can walk up.
I can walk down.
Can you walk?

7

Can you walk up?
Can you walk down?

8

Book 13

DOGS CAN

Pictures by

_____

I like dogs.

2

Dogs can run.

3

Dogs can jump.

4

33

Dogs can run in.

5

Dogs can walk.

6

Dogs can sit.

7

Can dogs read?

8

Book 14

I AM,
I CAN

Pictures by

_____

I am big.

2

A baby is little.

3

I can run.

4

I can sit.

5

I can jump up.

6

I can ride and ride.

7

I can read.

8

THE BIKE RIDE

The boy will walk to the house.

2

He will get a bike.

3

He will ride to my house.

4

I will get my bike. I will go, too.

5

I will ride my bike.
I will ride and ride.

6

We will ride up and down.

7

We will go and go.

8

MOTHER, FATHER, AND BABY GO

Father likes to sit.

2

Mother will get Father.

3

Mother and Father will get the baby.

4

Baby likes to go.

5

Mother and Father and the baby go.

6

Mother and Father run.
The baby cannot run.

7

The baby likes to sit.

8

PIG AND MOUSE

The pig has a box.
2

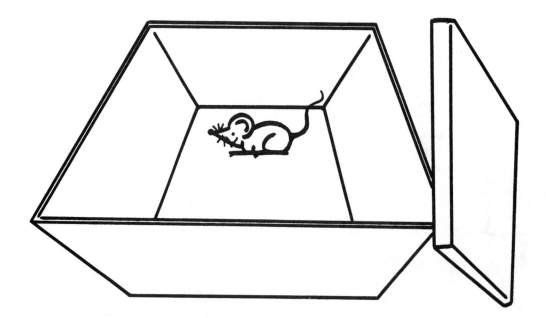

The mouse is in the box.

3

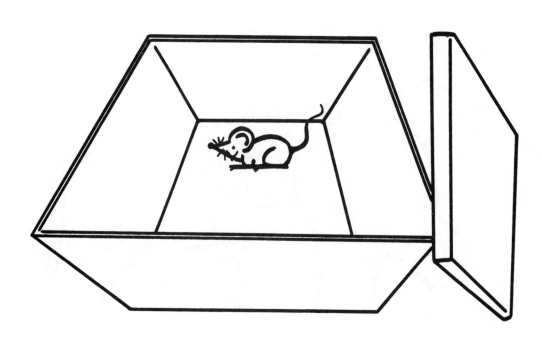

The mouse can get out of the box.

4

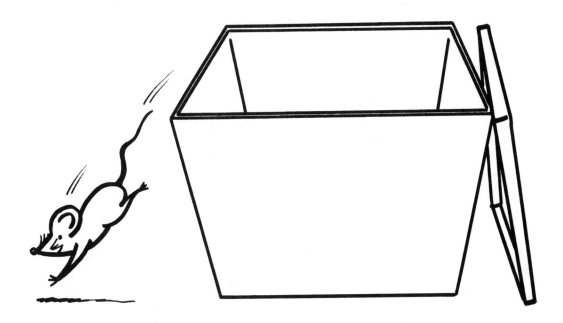

The mouse can run out of the box.

5

The mouse can get on a bike.
The mouse can ride up and down.

6

The pig can get on a bike.
The pig can ride up and down.

7

The pig and the mouse ride to my house.

8

SHE READS, HE READS

The girl likes to read.
She likes to read books.

2

She reads to the boy.

3

The boy likes the book.

4

The girl and the boy sit and read.

5

They read in the house.

6

They read out of the house.

7

They like to read.

8

THE BOOK

A mouse can run. A pig can run.

The dog has a book.

2

There is a mouse in the book.
There is a pig in the book.

3

The dog likes the book.

4

The dog reads the book.

5

He reads the book to the bear.

6

He reads the book to the rabbit.

7

He reads the book to the cat.

8

A RACE

The rabbit likes to run.
She runs and runs and runs.

2

The cat likes to run.
He runs and runs.

3

The rabbit wants to run.
The cat wants to run.
They want to run a race.

They walk to the house. They get on the line.
The dog will say, "Go!"

5

The dog says, "GO!"
The rabbit runs fast.
The cat runs fast.

6

They run fast.
The rabbit gets hot.
The cat gets hot.

7

They get wet.

8

A 1	is 1	big 1	little 1
Are 2	you 2	my 2	baby 2
No 2	Yes 2	My 2	You 3
are 3	not 3	mother 3	Run 6
run 6	In 6	Out 6	out 6
up 7	down 7	in 7	Hot 7
dog 7	Boys 8	Girls 8	ride 8
Ride 8	jump 8	Jump 8	and 8
girl 9	sat 9	on 9	the 9
swing 9	boy 9	rabbit 9	mouse 9

They	fell	I	like
9	9	10	10
dogs	can	Dogs	Big
10	10	10	10
Little	sit	to	The
10	10	10	11
got	box	am	a
11	11	12	12
read	Can	walk	. ?
12	12	12	
sun	fun	bun	pot
lot	side	hide	tide
pat	mat	hat	bike
hike	Mike	tan	man
pan	bit	fit	hit

will [15]	house [15]	He [15]	get [15]
bike [15]	go [15]	too [15]	We [15]
Father [16]	likes [16]	Mother [16]	Baby [16]
cannot [16]	pig [17]	has [17]	of [17]
She [18]	books [18]	reads [18]	book [18]
There [19]	bear [19]	cat [19]	wants [20]
race [20]	line [20]	say [20]	says [20]
day	set	pet	dig
may	let	met	wig
pay	net	big	fig

Sentence Strips

Cut apart and use after
Follow-up Activities Using Phonics (see page 7).

I ride my bike.	Go up, not down.
I like to hide.	You can run in the sun.
The man is tan.	The pot is not hot.
Mike hit the pan.	You sat on my hat.
You can hike.	The swing is fun.
You can sit on my side.	The boy got a lot.
The dog bit the man.	I like my bike.
I bit the bun.	He met my pet.